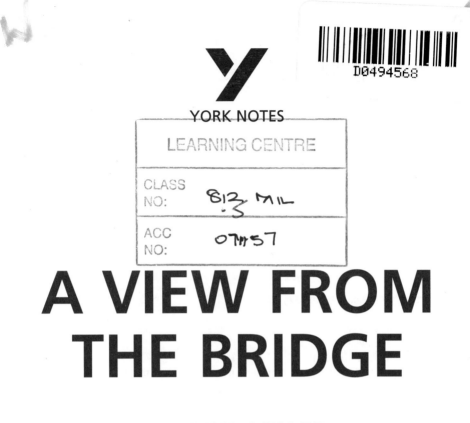

YORK NOTES

A VIEW FROM THE BRIDGE

ARTHUR MILLER

NOTES BY SHAY DALY

 Longman

 York Press

YORK PRESS
322 Old Brompton Road, London SW5 9JH

PEARSON EDUCATION LIMITED
Edinburgh Gate, Harlow,
Essex CM20 2JE, United Kingdom
Associated companies, branches and representatives throughout the world

First published 1997
This new and fully revised edition first published 2002
Sixth impression 2006

10 9 8 7 6

ISBN-10: 0-582-50624-7
ISBN-13: 978-0-582-50624-4

Designed by Michelle Cannatella
Illustrated by Chris Price
Phototypeset by Gem Graphics, Trenance, Mawgan Porth, Cornwall
Produced by Pearson Education Asia Limited, Hong Kong

CONTENTS

PREFACE

York Notes are designed to give you a broader perspective on works of literature studied at GCSE and equivalent levels. With examination requirements changing in the twenty-first century, we have made a number of significant changes to this new series. We continue to help students to reach their own interpretations of the text but York Notes now have important extra-value new features.

You will discover that York Notes are genuinely interactive. The new **Checkpoint** features make sure that you can test your knowledge and broaden your understanding. You will also be directed to excellent websites, books and films where you can follow up ideas for yourself.

The **Resources** section has been updated and an entirely new section has been devoted to how to improve your grade. Careful reading and application of the principles laid out in the Resources section guarantee improved performance.

The **Detailed summaries** include an easy-to-follow skeleton structure of the story-line, while the section on **Language and style** has been extended to offer an in-depth discussion of the writer's techniques.

The Contents page shows the structure of this study guide. However, there is no need to read from the beginning to the end as you would with a novel, play or poem. Use the Notes in the way that suits you. Our aim is to help you with your understanding of the work, not to dictate how you should learn.

Our authors are practising English teachers and examiners who have used their experience to offer a whole range of **Examiner's secrets** – useful hints to encourage exam success.

The General Editor of this series is John Polley, Senior GCSE Examiner and former Head of English at Harrow Way Community School, Andover.

The author of these Notes is Shay Daly. After leaving school to become a professional actor, Shay studied English and Drama at De La Salle College and Manchester University. He has taught in Manchester for over twenty years, first as Head of Drama and now as Head of English at Barlow High School in Didsbury. He is a Senior Examiner and Moderator for an Examination Board.

The text used in these Notes is the Penguin Twentieth-Century Classics Edition, 1961.

INTRODUCTION

HOW TO STUDY A PLAY

Though it may seem obvious, remember that a play is written to be performed before an audience. Ideally, you should see the play live on stage. A film or video recording is next best, though neither can capture the enjoyment of being in a theatre and realising that your reactions are part of the performance.

There are six aspects of a play:

❶ THE PLOT: a play is a story whose events are carefully organised by the playwright in order to show how a situation can be worked out

❷ THE CHARACTERS: these are the people who have to face this situation. Since they are human they can be good or bad, clever or stupid, likeable or detestable, etc. They may change too!

❸ THE THEMES: these are the underlying messages of the play, e.g. jealousy can cause the worst of crimes; ambition can bring the mightiest low

❹ THE SETTING: this concerns the time and place that the author has chosen for the play

❺ THE LANGUAGE: the writer uses a certain style of expression to convey the characters and ideas

❻ STAGING AND PERFORMANCE: the type of stage, the lighting, the sound effects, the costumes, the acting styles and delivery must all be decided

Work out the choices the dramatist has made in the first four areas, and consider how a director might balance these choices to create a live performance.

The purpose of these York Notes is to help you understand what the play is about and to enable you to make your own interpretation. Do not expect the study of a play to be neat and easy: plays are chosen for examination purposes, not written for them!

DID YOU KNOW?

Arthur Miller wrote three endings to conclude *A View from the Bridge*. At the end of one French production Eddie kills himself.

AUTHOR – LIFE AND WORKS

1915 Arthur Miller born 17 October in New York.

1934 Enrols at the University of Michigan

1938–40 Works for Federal Theatre Project

1940 Marries Mary Slattery

1944 *The Man who had all the Luck* performed

1947 *All My Sons* produced

1948 Studies the lives of the longshoremen in Brooklyn

1949 Writes *Death of a Salesman*

1950 Adapts Ibsen's *An Enemy of the People*. Miller summoned before the House of Un-American Activities Committee to name those he was associated with at left-wing meetings in the 1930s. Refused and was fined. Later the fine was quashed by the Supreme Court

1953 Writes *The Crucible*

1956 Divorces Mary Slattery and marries Marilyn Monroe

1956 Completes the two-act version of *A View from the Bridge*

1961 Monroe and Miller are divorced

1964 Writes *After the Fall*

1977 *The Archbishop's Calling* is produced

1980 Writes *The American Clock*

1994 Writes the play *Broken Glass*

CONTEXT

1918 First World War ends

1920s The boom years in America

1929 Wall Street Crash

1930s The Great Depression

1939–45 Second World War

1941 Pearl Harbour attacked by Japan

1945 Atomic bombs dropped on Hiroshima and on Nagasaki by the Americans

1950s The House of Un-American Activities Committee investigates Communist sympathisers. Anti-Communist feeling stirred up by Senator Joseph McCarthy

1954 McCarthy discredited and anti-Communist feelings began to moderate

1962 Marilyn Monroe dies. Cuban missile crisis

1963 John F. Kennedy assassinated

1988–91 Communism collapses in Eastern Europe

SETTING AND BACKGROUND

EXPLOITATION OF ITALIAN IMMIGRANTS

In the 1940s, Arthur Miller spent two years working with Italians in the shipyards of Brooklyn and was thus able to study the social background of the lives of the dockworkers in that area. He discovered that the people were very poorly paid and he felt that they were being used by the owners. Many of the workers were illegal immigrants and were being exploited by the very people who helped bring them to America. They looked after the immigrants until such time as they had paid for their services and then they were left to fend for themselves.

During this time Arthur Miller had close associations with the families of the dockworkers. In his **autobiography** *Time Bends* he narrates that a friend told him about a dream he had about an attraction he felt for his cousin. When Arthur Miller interpreted the dream as an indication that the man might have wanted an incestuous relationship with the girl the man was horrified and refused to accept that there might be any truth in what Arthur Miller was saying.

The playwright observed that the dockers waited every day on the waterfront in the hope that they would get a job. He soon realised that this practice was prevalent in Sicily when he visited the country a few years after his experiences in the docks of Brooklyn. Arthur Miller found the practices unacceptable. He saw them as unfair and humiliating. It gave the bosses far too much control over the men and, because of this, created situations which were open to corruption.

It was during this time that Arthur Miller heard the story of a longshoreman who had betrayed two of his own relatives to the Immigration Authorities because he was not happy about the relationship between one of the immigrants and his niece.

All of this was raw material for the play *A View from the Bridge*. At first Arthur Miller wrote a **verse play** in the form of a Greek **tragedy** or **melodrama** in one Act. In 1956 he wrote the **full-length prose** version that we know today.

CHECK THE BOOK

Arthur Miller's **autobiography** *Time Bends* (1987) should be read for the insight it gives into the origin of many of the plays and for his motivation for writing them.

CHECK THE BOOK

Arthur Miller (1982) by Neil Carson is an excellent introduction to the works of Arthur Miller.

EXAMINER'S SECRET

You will gain more credit if you show you have some understanding of the play in its historical context.

THE SETTING

The play is set in Red Hook in Brooklyn. Red Hook is a slum area inhabited by the Carbones and their neighbours. Alfieri, the lawyer, views the drama from Brooklyn Bridge. Most of the action takes place in the Carbones' living room and dining room but some scenes are located in the street outside their house. It is important that we see the Carbones as part of the wider community, especially towards the end of the play when their private tragedy becomes part of the public stage.

THEMES IN MILLER'S PLAYS

Arthur Miller is now regarded as one of the world's greatest dramatists. In his plays he explores the struggles of the ordinary man against authority and insurmountable odds. His examination of the past and how it can haunt the present and the future is a powerful tool in his armoury when writing about the thin line every person walks through life. While examining and exposing human weaknesses he also shows an understanding of the deep-lying emotions within every human being.

Now take a break!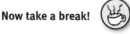

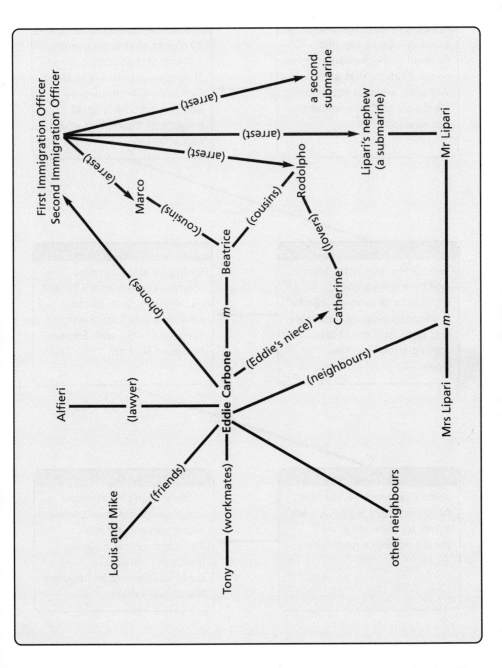

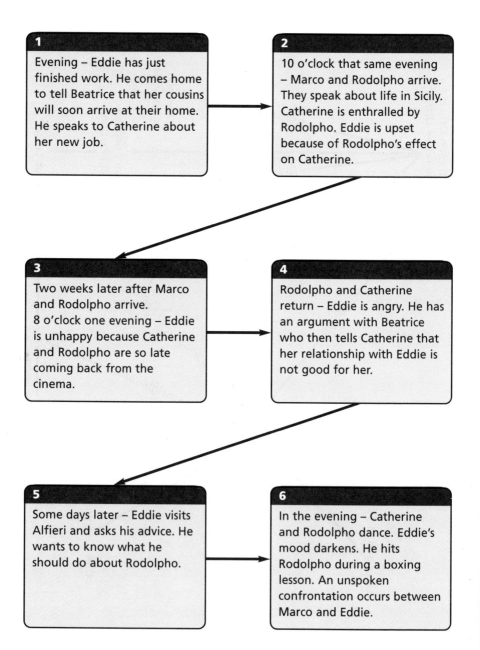

1
Evening – Eddie has just finished work. He comes home to tell Beatrice that her cousins will soon arrive at their home. He speaks to Catherine about her new job.

2
10 o'clock that same evening – Marco and Rodolpho arrive. They speak about life in Sicily. Catherine is enthralled by Rodolpho. Eddie is upset because of Rodolpho's effect on Catherine.

3
Two weeks later after Marco and Rodolpho arrive.
8 o'clock one evening – Eddie is unhappy because Catherine and Rodolpho are so late coming back from the cinema.

4
Rodolpho and Catherine return – Eddie is angry. He has an argument with Beatrice who then tells Catherine that her relationship with Eddie is not good for her.

5
Some days later – Eddie visits Alfieri and asks his advice. He wants to know what he should do about Rodolpho.

6
In the evening – Catherine and Rodolpho dance. Eddie's mood darkens. He hits Rodolpho during a boxing lesson. An unspoken confrontation occurs between Marco and Eddie.

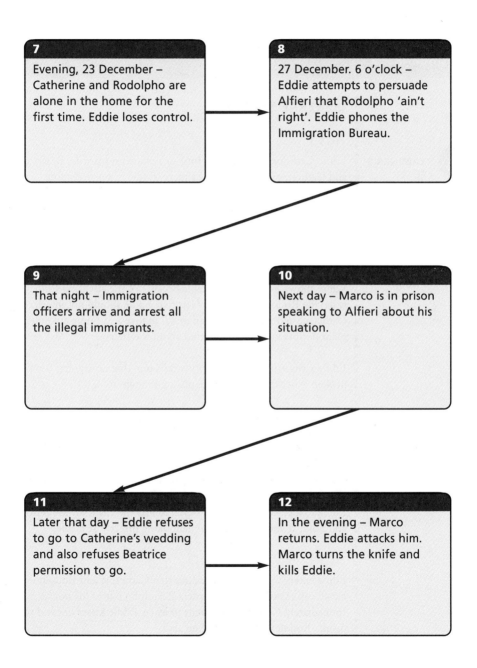

7

Evening, 23 December – Catherine and Rodolpho are alone in the home for the first time. Eddie loses control.

8

27 December. 6 o'clock – Eddie attempts to persuade Alfieri that Rodolpho 'ain't right'. Eddie phones the Immigration Bureau.

9

That night – Immigration officers arrive and arrest all the illegal immigrants.

10

Next day – Marco is in prison speaking to Alfieri about his situation.

11

Later that day – Eddie refuses to go to Catherine's wedding and also refuses Beatrice permission to go.

12

In the evening – Marco returns. Eddie attacks him. Marco turns the knife and kills Eddie.

SUMMARIES

GENERAL SUMMARY

ACT I

Eddie Carbone lives in Red Hook, a slum, with his wife, Beatrice, and Catherine who is Beatrice's niece. Eddie is worried about Catherine leaving the security of the house. Beatrice awaits the arrival of her cousins, Marco and Rodolpho, who are illegal immigrants from Italy. Eddie tells Beatrice and Catherine that they must never talk about the cousins outside the house.

Marco and Rodolpho arrive to a warm welcome. Soon, however, Eddie shows he is uncomfortable because of the attention Catherine is paying Rodolpho. Beatrice feels that Eddie should not interfere. Catherine and Rodolpho begin to fall in love and Eddie attempts to plant doubts in Catherine's mind about the Italian.

Eddie visits Alfieri but the lawyer tells him that no law has been broken other than the laws regulating immigration.

At home Eddie listens to the Italians telling Catherine and Beatrice about their life at home in Italy. Eddie turns on Rodolpho and accuses him of not behaving according to the American code. He tells Rodolpho that he is not happy about the relationship he has established with Catherine. Rodolpho allows Eddie to show him how to box. Eddie hits him and Marco intervenes by challenging Eddie to a chair-lifting contest. Marco lifts the chair without effort and holds it above his head while looking directly at Eddie.

ACT II

Eddie enters the house and realises that Catherine and Rodolpho have been making love. He orders Rodolpho out of his house. Immediately Catherine threatens to leave. Eddie kisses her and then insults Rodolpho by kissing him also.

Eddie phones the Immigration Authorities to inform them that Marco and Rodolpho are illegal immigrants. He then returns home where he discovers that Catherine is determined to marry Rodolpho. The Immigration Officers enter and arrest Marco and Rodolpho and also the two other illegal immigrants who have just arrived. Catherine, Beatrice and, finally, Marco realise that Eddie has informed on the brothers. Marco spits at Eddie who threatens to kill him. Eddie protests his innocence.

Alfieri persuades Marco to promise not to attack Eddie. Without this promise he cannot arrange bail for the brothers. Marco will have to return to Italy but Rodolpho's marriage to Catherine will allow the younger cousin to stay in America, legally.

Beatrice is making arrangements to go to Catherine's wedding when Eddie tells her that if she goes she must not return to the house. Rodolpho returns and tries to persuade Eddie to leave because Marco is coming for revenge. Beatrice now confronts Eddie with the truth about his feelings for Catherine but Eddie will not accept her accusations.

Eddie accuses Marco of lying about him. Marco attacks Eddie who pulls out a knife. Marco turns the knife on Eddie and he dies as Catherine and Beatrice attempt to comfort him.

Alfieri concludes the play by telling the audience that it is better to settle for less than the whole truth but that he does admire a man who allows himself to be 'wholly known' (Act II, p. 85).

? DID YOU KNOW?
Arthur Miller's most successful play *Death of a Salesman* was written in six weeks.

Now take a break!

DETAILED SUMMARIES

PART ONE [pp. 11–53] – Setting the scene

CHECKPOINT 1

What is the definition of justice?

❶ Alfieri tells the audience that justice and the law are often administered separately in Red Hook.

❷ Eddie upsets Catherine by criticising her clothes and behaviour.

❸ Beatrice is nervous because of the arrival of her cousins who are illegal immigrants.

❹ Eddie is unhappy when Catherine tells him she has a job.

❺ Beatrice tells of Vinny Bolzano who informed on illegal immigrants.

❻ The cousins, Marco and Rodolpho, arrive.

❼ Eddie shows hostility towards Rodolpho.

DID YOU KNOW?

Miller introduces Alfieri as a type of modern Greek **chorus**, as someone who helps create a framework for the play.

The play opens with Alfieri's thoughtful analysis of the situation in Red Hook. He speaks in an easy conversational style. The story is told in a series of **flashbacks** and Alfieri controls the thread.

Alfieri, a lawyer, enters and immediately creates the **atmosphere** – the atmosphere of a place where crime was once set into the very fabric of the neighbourhood. He tells the audience about the importance of justice but, he says, justice is often administered outside rather than inside the law. He mentions Al Capone and Frankie Yale and, later, Caesar himself to emphasise that the present case he is about to handle may not be very different from many of the 'bloody course[s]' (p. 12) that have occurred throughout the history of Italy. He is also stating that the conflict, like all the others, is beyond the power of anybody to stop it. Most of the time, however, there is a veneer of respectability. Most of the time people are quite civilised.

Alfieri introduces Eddie Carbone. Eddie, the **protagonist**, is an unsophisticated longshoreman. His language and that of Catherine and Beatrice betray a **colloquialism** that is powerful but often hides more than it reveals.

Eddie enters and speaks to Catherine, his niece. At first he is very proud of the way she looks 'like one of them girls that went to college' (p. 13) but he is soon irritated because, he feels, her skirt is too short, and her walk is provocative.

The relationship between Catherine and Eddie appears open and sincere but there is some uneasiness in the air. Catherine desperately craves Eddie's approval and is very upset when he criticises her clothes. The attraction between the two **characters** is strong and this causes Eddie to feel pleasure and pain when he looks at Catherine and observes her changing appearance. He feels pain because he wonders how the local young men react when they see her.

Eddie now informs Beatrice that her cousins have arrived from Italy. This is a tense, exciting moment for Beatrice. She is delighted that they have arrived but anxious for their safety. Eddie, however, is confident and shows that he is in charge of the situation. Eddie jokes with Beatrice but there is a hint that he is not totally at ease with the situation. She is afraid of the consequences if they are caught but she is very eager to meet the two men. She worries that the house is not as it should be. Eddie takes control and attempts to calm her but then adds to her tension and sense of guilt when he reminds her that she promised to cover the chair. Almost immediately he introduces a sense of perspective when he assures Beatrice that she is saving her

CHECKPOINT 2

How do you explain Eddie's contradictory feelings for Catherine?

CHECKPOINT 3

Why does the imminent arrival of Marco and Rodolpho cast a gloom over the family?

EXAMINER'S SECRET

When revising, examine the relevance of the title: *A View from the Bridge*.

cousins' lives. Again, however, Eddie accuses Beatrice that she is always prepared to help her relatives at his expense. But after all this he succeeds in persuading Beatrice that he is a very generous person.

Beatrice and Catherine are nervous before telling Eddie that Catherine wishes to accept the job she has been offered. Catherine wants support from Beatrice before she will tell Eddie that she has a job. Eddie disapproves of the fact that Catherine wants to work. Immediately Eddie raises objections. He says he wants her to complete her education, he doesn't care for the neighbourhood she would be working in and he doesn't like the sailors and plumbers with whom she would be in contact. He wants her to be able to rise above her present situation – to be in a different class.

CHECKPOINT 4

How does Eddie react to the news that Catherine is going to work?

When alone with Eddie, Beatrice attempts to persuade him to allow Catherine her freedom. She is angry when he rejects her advice. However Beatrice shows how forceful she can be when she persuades Eddie to allow Catherine to work. Catherine responds very emotionally but Eddie attempts to dampen her spirits when he suggests that not everybody she works with will be trustworthy.

For a moment Eddie allows them to be a family. He shows affection for Catherine when he calls her 'madonna' (p. 20) before giving her permission to go to work. He also makes it clear that he will feel a great sense of loss when she goes. There is laughter and good humour when Eddie talks about his work. Catherine's unselfishness shines through when she forgets her own news in order to concentrate on Eddie's important announcement – that the cousins have arrived.

The imminent arrival of the cousins casts a gloom over the three of them – the **atmosphere** changes again. Beatrice asks the time and the conversation turns to the cousins' arrival. Catherine worries about hiding the cousins' identity – they might be seen entering and leaving the house. Eddie insists that it does not matter what people think, it is important that Catherine, Beatrice and himself do not talk about the cousins to anybody. Eddie prompts Beatrice to tell the story of Vinny Bolzano. Vinny Bolzano informed the Authorities about an uncle who was staying with the family. When the family discovered that Vinny was the informer they treated him as an outcast and he had to leave the area. All three **characters** show their revulsion at the betrayal. The **irony** will not be lost on the audience at the end of the play. Eddie then outlines the way the illegal immigrants are looked after until they have paid their dues to those who shipped them in.

There is a quiet moment when Eddie turns to Catherine and says that he never expected her to grow up. While she is out of the room Eddie asks Beatrice why she is always angry with him recently. Beatrice denies this and repeats the word 'mad' (p. 25) three times – perhaps indicating that she worries about Eddie's sanity. Catherine returns with a cigar and lights it for Eddie.

Marco and Rodolpho arrive and are escorted to Eddie's house by Tony who makes it quite clear that they are now on their own but they must go to work. Alfieri tells the audience that Eddie does what is required and no more.

Beatrice, Catherine and Eddie give a warm welcome to the cousins. Marco assures Eddie that they will not outstay their welcome because he realises that the house is small. Catherine notices the fact that there is a marked difference in the colour of the two men. To her annoyance, Eddie interrupts. He tells Marco and Rodolpho that they

CHECKPOINT 5

Why is the story about Vinny Bolzano, the informer, important?

EXAMINER'S SECRET

Always support your comments with details from the text.

CHECKPOINT 6

Why does Eddie feel uncomfortable when Rodolpho begins to sing?

DID YOU KNOW?

Longshoremen would wait in Red Hook at 4:30 in the morning hoping to get work.

have to work on the piers, work they have never undertaken before. The men describe the work in Italy, Marco seriously but Rodolpho laughing all the time. Rodolpho paints a picture of a poor peasant town. Marco, however, talks about his own situation. He has a family and wife to support and they have very little to eat. He will stay, he says, for six years. He is delighted when Eddie tells him how much they will earn and asks Beatrice if they can stay for a few months in her house because that will enable him to send more money back to his family. Catherine asks Rodolpho if he is married. He replies that he is too poor to marry. Unlike Marco, he wants to stay in America and have a powerful motorcycle. Rodolpho's vibrant good humour and comic turn of phrase is appreciated by Beatrice and by Catherine. Eddie, however, does not find him humorous and he attempts to prevent him establishing a relationship with Catherine who obviously finds Rodolpho attractive. Rodolpho's singing of *Paper Doll* makes Eddie feel very uncomfortable. Indeed the lyrics could be a comment on the way he feels about Catherine. He rudely interrupts the singer by threatening him that people will be suspicious. He continues his belligerent behaviour by insisting that Catherine change her shoes.

Themes of law and justice

Law and justice are important themes that run through the play. Alfieri touches on these themes in his opening speech. The law is looked on with suspicion but justice is very important. Justice, Alfieri says, was often dispensed by breaking the law and he feels that seeking total justice is an uncomfortable way to live. He, himself, is happy to 'settle for half' (p. 12).

He senses that there is a timeless quality about this story. Perhaps, he thinks, this very struggle for justice was observed by a lawyer two thousand years ago.

Now take a break!

WHO SAYS ...?

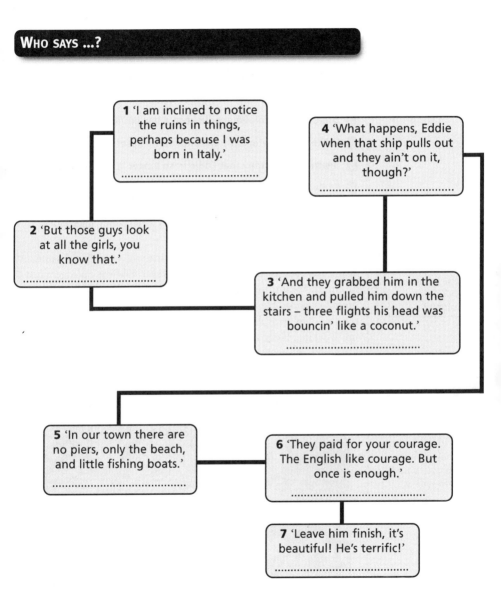

1 'I am inclined to notice the ruins in things, perhaps because I was born in Italy.'

....

2 'But those guys look at all the girls, you know that.'

....

3 'And they grabbed him in the kitchen and pulled him down the stairs – three flights his head was bouncin' like a coconut.'

....

4 'What happens, Eddie when that ship pulls out and they ain't on it, though?'

....

5 'In our town there are no piers, only the beach, and little fishing boats.'

....

6 'They paid for your courage. The English like courage. But once is enough.'

....

7 'Leave him finish, it's beautiful! He's terrific!'

....

Check your answers on p. 69.

PART TWO [pp. 33–45] – Rodolpho and Catherine

1 Alfieri comments on Eddie's troubled future.

2 Eddie disapproves of Rodolpho's activities.

3 Eddie feels Rodolpho should keep a low profile.

4 Catherine's relationship with Rodolpho upsets Eddie.

5 Beatrice is unhappy that Eddie is no longer 'a husband' to her.

6 Eddie tells Catherine that Rodolpho is using her to become an American citizen.

7 Beatrice talks to Catherine about her relationship with Eddie.

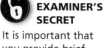

CHECKPOINT 7

Why is Eddie jealous of Rodolpho?

6 EXAMINER'S SECRET

It is important that you provide brief quotations to ensure that they do not overshadow your own comments.

Alfieri enters and suggests that Eddie's life will never be the same again. His routine has been changed forever. Eddie is on edge when he enters. He is upset that Rodolpho is spending so much of his time on public show. He does not like the fact that Rodolpho is singing on the ships and he feels that the Italian should stay at home when he is not working. He is also unhappy about the amount of time that Catherine is spending with Rodolpho.

Eddie shows his irritation, because Catherine and Rodolpho have not returned from the cinema. Despite Beatrice's effort to calm the situation, Eddie will not be persuaded. He regards Rodolpho 'like a weird' (p. 35) and something other than a (real) man. He suggests that the Italian is rather effeminate.

Beatrice makes it clear that she thinks Eddie is jealous of Rodolpho. She then asks Eddie why he has not made love to her for over three months. He, however, refuses to discuss the matter and returns instead to the issue of Catherine and Rodolpho. Beatrice remarks that Eddie's interest is unhealthy.

Beatrice is now determined to force Eddie to face some unpleasant facts. She attempts to discuss the flaws in their own relationship but Eddie instead returns to the subject of Rodolpho and Catherine. The tension created between Eddie and Beatrice is too much for Eddie and he walks out. When Eddie meets Mike and Louis they tell him how much they admire Marco for his work rate and how amusing they find Rodolpho.

EXAMINER'S SECRET

Read all parts of the question carefully to ensure you answer them fully.

CHECKPOINT 8

What is Eddie's real reason for suggesting that Rodolpho is 'like a weird' (Act I, p. 35).

Catherine and Rodolpho return from the cinema and Eddie shows his disapproval. Rodolpho exits when Eddie indicates that he wishes to speak to Catherine on her own. He tells her how much he misses her and also that he is certain Rodolpho is only going out with her because he wants to become an American citizen when she marries him. Catherine does not believe him but nevertheless Eddie pursues

HARROW COLLEGE
HH Learning Centre
Lowlands Road, Harrow
Middx. HA1 3AQ
020 8909 6520

his defamation of the Italian's character. He says that as soon as she marries him he will become an American citizen and then he will divorce her. Catherine is now very upset. Beatrice enters and angrily insists that Eddie leave her alone. Eddie walks off into the house.

CHECKPOINT 9

Why is Catherine upset by the suggestion that Rodolpho wants to become an American citizen?

Eddie's hostility increases

The undercurrent of the exchange between Eddie and his workmates sets him on edge. This conversation, the previous accusation by Beatrice and now the excited laughter of Catherine as she returns with Rodolpho are all frustrations that Eddie allows to fuel his inner hostility. He maligns Rodolpho to Catherine when he questions the young man's motives for wanting a relationship with her. Catherine breaks down in the face of his onslaught and attempts to shut him out.

CHECKPOINT 10

Why does Beatrice force Catherine to think about her relationship with Eddie?

Beatrice talks seriously to Catherine about her relationship with Eddie. She says that Eddie will always find something wrong with any boy who is interested in her. She tells Catherine that she must be more independent, more grown-up. She makes it quite clear to Catherine that she is a grown woman and Eddie is a grown man and, because of this, she must behave differently from now on. Catherine assures her that she will but she is afraid because her world is no longer secure.

 DID YOU KNOW?

During one production of *A View from the Bridge* one man attended every performance. He said he knew the family onstage and that they lived next door to him.

Beatrice, quietly, takes control. She asks questions and makes statements, all of which eventually force Catherine to confront some uncomfortable truths about her relationship with Eddie. The suggestion is that Catherine's attachment to Eddie prevents her breaking free from him. Beatrice does not wish to hurt Catherine but she is insistent.

Now take a break!

WHO SAYS …?

1 'A man works, raises his family, goes bowling, eats, gets old, and then he dies.'

....

4 'He blesses you, and you don't talk to him hardly.'

....

2 'Marco goes around like a man; nobody kids Marco.'

....

3 'But he's a kid yet, y'know? He – he's just a kid, that's all.'

....

ABOUT WHOM?

5 'Yeah, I mean, he's always makin' like remarks, like, y'know?'

....

6 'what are you going to do with yourself?'

....

7 'Just give him to understand; you don't have to fight, you're just – You're a woman, that's all'

....

Check your answers on p. 69.

PART THREE [pp. 45–58] – Eddie's mood darkens

1. Eddie attempts, unsuccessfully, to persuade Alfieri that Rodolpho is breaking the law.

2. Eddie tells Rodolpho he is breaking the American code of morality.

3. Catherine flirts with Rodolpho.

4. Eddie hits Rodolpho while showing him how to box.

5. Marco shows his superior strength and power over Eddie.

EXAMINER'S SECRET

Look at the different layers of meaning in **dialogue**.

CHECKPOINT 11

What does Eddie want Alfieri to do for him when they first meet?

CHECKPOINT 12

Why does Alfieri feel helpless when listening to Eddie?

Alfieri is puzzled when Eddie comes to see him and Alfieri now becomes one of the **characters** in the drama itself. He tries to explain to Eddie that no crime has been committed even though Eddie may think that Rodolpho wants to marry Catherine in order to make him a legal immigrant.

Eddie passionately states his case. He believes that Alfieri should be capable of proving that Rodolpho is breaking the law. Alfieri points out that Eddie is merely supposing what is inside Rodolpho's mind. Eddie attempts to prove that Rodolpho is not a real man – 'he ain't right' (p. 46). He states that his hair is platinum, he sings in a high voice like a girl, he can cut out dresses and he is laughed at when he goes to work. These are statements of a desperate man who is blinkered to reason.

Eddie's frustration

The audience now hears Eddie say what is, perhaps, his most significant pronouncement so far:

'But I know what they're laughin' at, and when I think of that guy layin' his hands on her I could – I mean it's eatin' me out, Mr Alfieri, because I struggled for that girl. And now he comes in my house and –'   (p. 47).

Eddie's frustration is embodied in these lines. He feels a desperation which he does not fully verbalise but it is possible that the audience can sense what he is really saying – that Catherine is rejecting Eddie who is a real man and a man who 'struggled' for her, unlike this effeminate boy.

CHECKPOINT 13

What, according to Eddie, is the American code and why is Rodolpho breaking the code?

Eddie is quick to dismiss Alfieri's suggestion that the only point of law that can be addressed is that of illegal immigration. He gives the impression that the very idea is against his principles. Alfieri's main concern is that Eddie is too involved with Catherine. He attempts to tell him tactfully when he explains that Eddie loves Catherine 'too much' (p. 48).

Eddie voices his desperate feeling of helplessness. Suddenly the audience feels that Eddie may be forcing himself to behave in a manner he may regret.

Alfieri feels helpless in the face of Eddie's desperation. He knows that Eddie is about to destroy himself and, perhaps, those near to him.

Beatrice and Catherine create a scene of harmonious domesticity as they talk to the men about life back in Italy. However, the undercurrent of Eddie's anger is sensed on every occasion he speaks to Rodolpho. Eddie controls and then destroys the relaxed mood of the family. Marco and Rodolpho relate some more details about their lives in Italy and we see how little Catherine and Eddie know about their cousins. Marco is happy that he can send money to his family but he makes it clear how much he misses his wife and children. Eddie compounds Marco's misery when he suggests that Marco's wife might be unfaithful. Rodolpho tells Eddie that there is a very strict code of morality in his country.

CHECKPOINT 14

Identify Alfieri's function in the play.

DID YOU KNOW?

Beatrice is not related to Catherine except through marriage.

CHECKPOINT 15

How are we made aware that Marco is the most powerful character at the end of Act I?

CHECKPOINT 16

Look at Marco's behaviour and ask yourself why he is stronger than Eddie.

EXAMINER'S SECRET

The award of a 'C' grade demands clear understanding of the dramatists' ideas.

Eddie is quick to seize the opportunity to turn the conversation to his advantage. He pointedly tells Rodolpho that the American code is no less strict than it is in Italy, and that Rodolpho himself is breaking this code in the cavalier way he has been taking Catherine out without his permission. Eddie repeats his assertion that Rodolpho should be working, not having a good time. Marco supports Eddie.

Beatrice encourages Catherine's show of independence when the girl asks Rodolpho to dance. It now becomes very important to Eddie that he assert himself over Rodolpho. He sneers at the Italian's ability to cook, inferring that it is not manly. He follows this with further comments on his ability to sing and make dresses. Eddie reflects darkly that Rodolpho's abilities do not qualify him for work on the dockyards. He is careful, however, not to criticise Rodolpho too openly. Instead he comments on his own shortcomings compared to the skills of Rodolpho. Eddie tears his newspaper in two thus making the point that he, a real man, could quite easily break Rodolpho if he so wished.

Eddie then attempts to show Rodolpho how to box. The encounter ends with Eddie landing a punch which staggers Rodolpho. Catherine is unhappy about this and so is Marco. He challenges Eddie to a chair-lifting competition. Eddie accepts but fails. Marco easily lifts the chair above his head and there is a tension between them as Eddie realises that Marco is warning him.

Trial of strength

The trial of strength is full of tension and **pathos**. While Eddie 'teaches' Rodolpho to box, the tension is shown through the reactions of the others:

- Beatrice, after her initial alarm, sees only what she considers friendly rivalry.
- Catherine is fearful for Rodolpho's safety. She is showing that, if necessary, she will take sides.
- Marco is cautious at first but then decides to react. He sees Eddie's action as hostile and deliberately challenges him to a trial of strength.

This contest is important because it shows that, when it really matters, Marco will always be loyal to Rodolpho and also that he, Marco, will be the stronger if Eddie attempts to show further aggression towards either of the brothers.

EXAMINER'S SECRET

You will gain high marks if you develop your ideas fully.

Now take a break!

WHO SAYS ...?

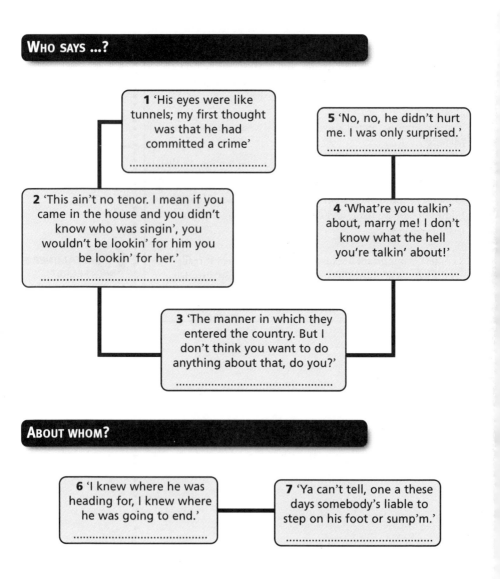

1 'His eyes were like tunnels; my first thought was that he had committed a crime'

....

5 'No, no, he didn't hurt me. I was only surprised.'

....

2 'This ain't no tenor. I mean if you came in the house and you didn't know who was singin', you wouldn't be lookin' for him you be lookin' for her.'

....

4 'What're you talkin' about, marry me! I don't know what the hell you're talkin' about!'

....

3 'The manner in which they entered the country. But I don't think you want to do anything about that, do you?'

....

ABOUT WHOM?

6 'I knew where he was heading for, I knew where he was going to end.'

....

7 'Ya can't tell, one a these days somebody's liable to step on his foot or sump'm.'

....

Check your answers on p. 69.

PART ONE [pp. 59–78] – Eddie informs on the cousins

❶ Catherine and Rodolpho are alone.

❷ Rodolpho attempts to persuade Catherine to break free from Eddie.

❸ Eddie returns and sees them coming out of the bedroom.

❹ Eddie tells Rodolpho to leave.

❺ He informs the Immigration Bureau of Marco and Rodolpho.

❻ The Immigration officers arrest Rodolpho and Marco.

❼ Marco suspects Eddie and spits in his face.

Alfieri introduces Act II in a good-humoured manner and ends his introduction with the loaded comment:

'Catherine told me later that this was the first time they had been alone together in the house.'   (p. 59)

The scene which follows is tender and loving. The audience sees the strength of feeling that Catherine and Rodolpho have for one another.

It is important to Catherine, however, that Rodolpho banishes her doubts, the seeds of which were laid earlier by Eddie. In response to her question Rodolpho answers that he would be 'crazy' (p. 60) if he took her back to Italy as his wife – that they would be going back to poverty. Catherine asks him if he would still marry her even if they went to live in Italy. Rodolpho makes it quite clear that he will not marry Catherine just so that he can become an American citizen. His intentions are genuine. He realises that the question has already been asked by Eddie and he is infuriated by this.

Rodolpho advises Catherine that she must break away from Eddie but she insists that she is the only person who really understands his needs and she does not know why she has to 'make a stranger out of him' (p. 62). She is reluctant to leave Eddie as he has been so good to her.

Rodolpho is very gentle, even sympathetic, but still strongly advises

EXAMINER'S SECRET
Practise skimming and scanning the extracts. This will save you time when looking for quotations.

CHECKPOINT 17

How does Rodolpho reassure Catherine that he will not use her to become an American citizen?

CHECKPOINT 18

What are Rodolpho's main strengths in this scene?

that Eddie must let her go. Catherine responds by showing her helplessness. She wants Rodolpho to make love to her and he leads her gently towards the bedroom.

Arthur Miller shows the audience that the relationship between Catherine and Rodolpho is stronger and more fulfilling than that between Beatrice and Eddie.

When Eddie enters unexpectedly, he is drunk and his anger rises as he sees what is happening between Catherine and Rodolpho.

EXAMINER'S SECRET
You should **not** spend too much time writing about the stage directions because this might distract you from the script.

Eddie is devastated and orders Rodolpho to leave. Catherine, instead, makes an effort to go but Eddie grabs her and kisses her. Rodolpho protests and tells him that she is going to be his wife. Eddie asks him what he is going to be and then shows his brutal nature when he kisses first Catherine and then Rodolpho. Catherine attacks her uncle who laughs at Rodolpho.

Eddie tells Catherine not to provoke him. The threat uttered by Eddie at the end of their struggle is too powerful to be ignored:

> Don't make me do nuttin', Catherine. Watch your step, submarine. By rights they oughta throw you back in the water. But I got pity for you.'   (p. 65)

Catherine and Rodolpho are left in no doubt that they will be powerless if Eddie decides to act.

Alfieri recognises the terrible change that has come over Eddie and the emptiness of his spirit. He knows, because of the inevitability of the **tragedy** that is about to happen, that he should do something to prevent it but he feels powerless to do so.

When Eddie tells Alfieri about the struggle it is significant that he omits to tell him about his kissing Catherine and Rodolpho. Alfieri also discovers from Eddie that Marco has not been informed of the incident between Rodolpho and Eddie. Eddie asks for the lawyer's help but once again Alfieri emphasises that the law has not been broken and therefore Eddie must accept the situation as it is and let nature take its course. If he does not, Alfieri insists, then he will be the loser.

Eddie now phones the Immigration Bureau, cautiously, and tells the officer that he wishes to report two illegal immigrants. He gives the address but refuses to give his name believing he will not be discovered.

Eddie refuses his friends' invitation to go bowling mainly because his mind is now completely focused on what has happened and on what is about to happen.

EXAMINER'S SECRET

You will achieve higher grades if you show empathy with the writer's ideas.

CHECKPOINT 19

How would you describe Beatrice's role in Act II?

Eddie returns home to discover Beatrice on her own. Marco and Rodolpho have moved upstairs to the rented accommodation and Catherine is with them. Beatrice is obviously very angry with Eddie and tells him that she does not want to hear any more from him about Rodolpho and Catherine. She tries desperately to make him see that he is becoming irrational. Eddie repeats his assertion that there is something not quite right about the Italian. Beatrice pleads with him to let Catherine go. Eddie tells her that he does not want any more discussion about what happens in his bedroom. Beatrice says that she accepts this.

She now tells Eddie that Catherine and Rodolpho are going to be married next week because of fears that Rodolpho might be arrested. Suddenly Eddie is crying and wants to leave the house. Catherine comes down and tells him that if he wants to be at the wedding it will take place on Saturday. Eddie tries to persuade her to go out and meet other boys but she is determined that the wedding will go ahead. Catherine is cold, almost calculating. She will not be diverted. She makes it quite clear to Eddie that she is marrying Rodolpho and that there is no way he can stop that happening. The audience now sees that at this moment in the play Catherine has frozen out all the love she had for Eddie.

 DID YOU KNOW?

Arthur Miller was arrested and fined because he would not inform on his friends who were Communist sympathisers.

Beatrice tells Eddie that Marco and Rodolpho are sharing rooms with two other illegal immigrants upstairs. Eddie is distraught when he discovers that Lipari's nephew is in the house with Marco and Rodolpho and says that Beatrice should get the men out of the house. He worries that they might have been followed. He also worries about what their families might do to him if the immigrants are arrested. His betrayal now takes on a new dimension.

CHECKPOINT 20

Why is it **ironic** that Eddie is the one who betrays Marco and Rodolpho?

The conversation is interrupted by the arrival of the Immigration Officers. The Immigration Officers are direct and uncompromising despite their own Italian connections. As far as they are concerned the law is the law and transcends any patriotic feelings they might have. Immediately it is obvious that Beatrice and Catherine suspect that Eddie is responsible for this betrayal. Beatrice speaks to Eddie just three times but her words make it clear that any denial of responsibility for this act of betrayal will be useless.

The officers find four men upstairs and lead them out of the house. As he leaves, Marco spits in Eddie's face. Eddie threatens to kill Marco, who turns and accuses Eddie of stealing the food from his children. The neighbours turn away from Eddie as he protests his innocence.

DID YOU KNOW?

Illegal immigration is still a problem and innocent victims are still being used by their bosses to make huge profits.

No respect

Arthur Miller introduces a series of words and actions which show the audience how completely Eddie has lost the respect of those near to him. The most significant point is made by Marco when he spits in Eddie's face. His accusation, 'That one! I accuse that one!' (p. 77) is heard by the group outside. Lipari turns his back on Eddie, as do his friends Louis and Mike.

Now take a break!

WHO SAYS ...?

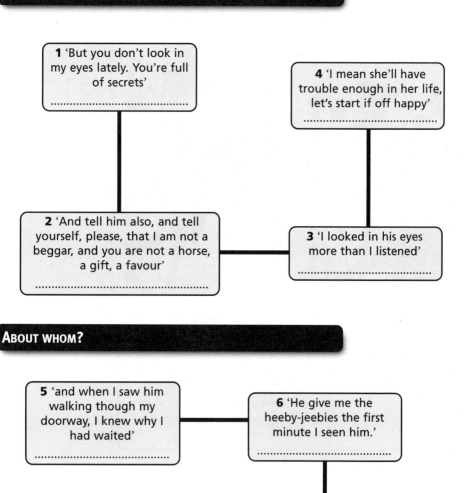

1 'But you don't look in my eyes lately. You're full of secrets'

....

2 'And tell him also, and tell yourself, please, that I am not a beggar, and you are not a horse, a gift, a favour'

....

3 'I looked in his eyes more than I listened'

....

4 'I mean she'll have trouble enough in her life, let's start if off happy'

....

ABOUT WHOM?

5 'and when I saw him walking though my doorway, I knew why I had waited'

....

6 'He give me the heeby-jeebies the first minute I seen him.'

....

7 'He's gonna take that back or I'll kill him!'

....

Check your answers on p. 69.

PART TWO [pp. 77–85] – Eddie dies

1. Alfieri attempts to persuade Marco not to kill Eddie.
2. Beatrice will not go to the wedding at Eddie's insistence.
3. Rodolpho tries to make peace.
4. Beatrice confronts Eddie with the truth about his feelings for Catherine.
5. Eddie demands that Marco give him back his name.
6. Eddie attacks Marco who then kills Eddie.
7. Alfieri mourns for Eddie but says it is better to 'settle for half' (p. 85).

Rodolpho, Marco and Catherine are in the reception room of the prison. Alfieri is waiting for Marco's assurance that he will not attack Eddie. Marco finds it difficult to agree because he feels Eddie should be made to pay for what he has done. Catherine and Rodolpho urge him to agree because they both want him at their wedding. However, Catherine condemns Eddie as she pleads with Marco not to do anything he will regret: 'To hell with Eddie. Nobody is gonna talk to him again if he lives to be a hundred' (p. 78).

Alfieri is again involved as the mediator when he attempts to persuade Marco that he must not take revenge. Marco is appealing to a justice that is above and beyond the law. Marco says:

'The law? All the law is not in a book.
…
He degraded my brother. My blood. He robbed my children, he mocks my work. I work to come here, mister!' (p. 79).

Alfieri points out that it is only God who delivers ultimate justice. Alfieri argues that he can, at least, work for six weeks before the trial. Marco finally agrees.

Arthur Miller now pushes the drama on relentlessly as the audience sees Beatrice preparing to go to the wedding and Eddie telling her that if she goes she must not come back to him. Catherine enters and

EXAMINER'S SECRET

It is important that you explore the characters, the situation and the dramatist's purpose.

suddenly attacks Eddie verbally. She tells him that he has no rights any more and when Beatrice explains that she cannot go to the wedding Catherine calls him a rat who bites people as they sleep.

Catherine builds on the venom she poured on Eddie previously when she makes it clear that she regards him as 'This rat!' (p. 81). She is clearly upset when Beatrice says that she cannot betray Eddie by going to the wedding. There is a finality to what Beatrice says: 'Now go, go to your wedding, Katie, I'll stay home. Go. God bless you, God bless your children' (p. 81).

Rodolpho enters. He tells Eddie that Marco is praying in the church before coming for Eddie. Beatrice is frightened and attempts to persuade Eddie to go away with her. The impasse between Eddie and Marco is now impossibly wide as we hear Eddie echo what Marco has said to Alfieri – he expects (or says he expects) Marco to apologise to him.

Rodolpho attempts to take all the blame for what has happened but Eddie merely brushes him aside. Rodolpho's warning to Eddie goes unheeded. Instead Eddie turns on the three of them to demand that his respect be returned to him. He has convinced himself that he is justified in asking for his self-respect.

The truth is out

At last, because he will not listen to reason, Beatrice says it openly: 'You want somethin' else, Eddie, and you can never have her!' (p. 83).

Catherine and Eddie are horrified but Beatrice follows on: 'The truth is not as bad as blood, Eddie! I'm tellin' you the truth – tell her good-bye for ever!' (p. 83).

Eddie will not accept this accusation and turns instead to face the challenge of Marco. This he can deal with and, indeed, will do so.

Marco enters and Eddie repeats his own name three times. He calls to Marco to give him his name to say that he, Marco, is a liar. If nothing else, Eddie has a tremendous capacity for self-delusion. His speech of self-justification is delivered with his family, friends and neighbours as audience. He calls on Marco to apologise to him for taking away his name. He lists the wrongs he has endured and also the hospitality he has freely given. Very deliberately Eddie forces the issue until he has created a confrontation from which Marco cannot withdraw. Marco calls him an animal.

Eddie lunges for Marco who strikes him and he falls. As Marco raises his foot Eddie draws a knife and lunges at him. Marco turns the knife and stabs Eddie. Eddie's final line indicates that he believes he has been wronged by Catherine and, therefore, by Rodolpho, Marco and even Beatrice. To the end he shows his capacity for self-delusion. Catherine protests that she didn't mean any harm. Eddie dies in Beatrice's arms.

Alfieri concludes by saying that it is better to settle for less than the whole truth, but while he believes this, he says he still loves Eddie because he allowed people to see him as he was – completely.

EXAMINER'S SECRET
Answers which provide an overview of the action will always impress.

Epilogue

Alfieri closes the play with a speech to the audience which tells us that he cannot help but be impressed by a man who did not compromise, 'he allowed himself to be wholly known' (p. 85).

He knows that it is better to 'settle for half' (p. 85) but he finds it necessary to convince himself.

His final line shows the contradictory nature of his feelings for Eddie: 'And so I mourn him – I admit it – with a certain … alarm' (p. 85).

CHECKPOINT 21

What does Alfieri mean when he says 'settle for half'?

Now take a break!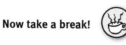

WHO SAYS ...?

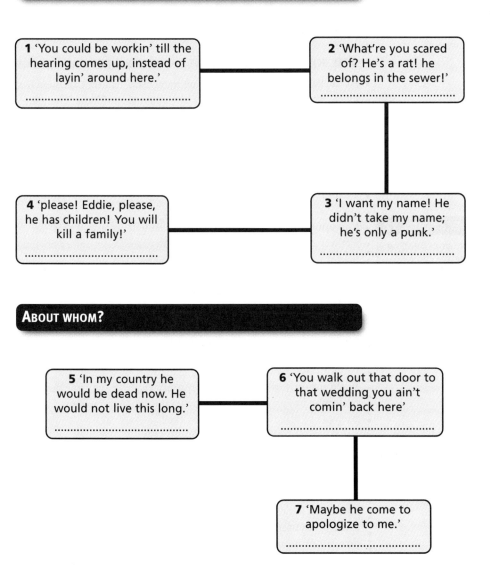

1 'You could be workin' till the hearing comes up, instead of layin' around here.'

....

2 'What're you scared of? He's a rat! he belongs in the sewer!'

....

4 'please! Eddie, please, he has children! You will kill a family!'

....

3 'I want my name! He didn't take my name; he's only a punk.'

....

ABOUT WHOM?

5 'In my country he would be dead now. He would not live this long.'

....

6 'You walk out that door to that wedding you ain't comin' back here'

....

7 'Maybe he come to apologize to me.'

....

Check your answers on p. 69.

COMMENTARY

THEMES

THE RELATIONSHIP BETWEEN EDDIE AND CATHERINE

At the beginning of the play we are immediately aware that there is a lively, intimate relationship between Catherine and Eddie. There are no barriers, as far as Catherine is concerned, and she is quite happy to show herself and her clothes to her uncle. Eddie is delighted at her beauty but because of this beauty he fears what other men will see. She will no longer be his girl; she will belong to the world – and the men – outside. Catherine is unhappy when Eddie does not fully accept the changes in her.

CHECKPOINT 22

How does Beatrice unsettle Eddie?

Catherine is further unsettled when Eddie will not accept that Catherine should take a job. His possessiveness is now more obvious than it was at the beginning. If Catherine goes out into the world of work she will consort with the male population every day. This unsettles Eddie. Beatrice comments about Eddie's relationship with Catherine on a number of occasions throughout the play. When Catherine leaves the room at the beginning Beatrice tries to make Eddie see that he is smothering Catherine and stifling the independence to which Catherine is entitled.

When the cousins arrive Eddie is quickly aware of the attraction Rodolpho has for Catherine and from this moment onwards Eddie attempts to place a barrier between them.

CHECKPOINT 23

How does Eddie react to Rodolpho?

Eddie feels out of his depth and cannot compete with the new worlds and experiences that Rodolpho is introducing to Catherine. This creates further conflict between the two men and also between Eddie and Catherine. Eddie can now see that she is no longer his possession because she is very attracted to this new life and her new exciting boyfriend. The audience can see that when Eddie makes a derogatory comment about Rodolpho he does so out of anger and frustration and that his attempts to keep Catherine for himself are unsuccessful.

There is a significant moment in Act I when Eddie asks Catherine if she likes Rodolpho. Her simple answer, 'Yeah. I like him' (p. 40), contains a rejection of her ties with Eddie and he is fully aware of this.

In a desperate attempt to force her to break her connection with Rodolpho, Eddie accuses Rodolpho of using Catherine to gain legal entry into the United States. This he hopes will force her to return to her dependence on him. However, Eddie's attempt to denigrate the Italian does not succeed and instead Catherine tells Eddie that Rodolpho's love for her is genuine. Eddie cannot accept what she says and immediately goes to Beatrice for support. Beatrice has no sympathy for him. Instead she accuses Eddie of not leaving Catherine alone and she is obviously losing patience with him.

Beatrice tries hard to tell Eddie that he must let Catherine go, that he must allow her freedom to have her relationship with Rodolpho. It is not until the end of the play that Beatrice says, quite specifically, that Eddie cannot have the relationship he wants with Catherine. But Eddie will not accept what she says – at least outwardly. However, the audience has no doubt that he knows what Beatrice has said is true. This is why he reacts in such an explosive way – as if to shut out the truth. Indeed, at this time the challenge from Marco is welcomed by Eddie as a way to destroy his awareness of the truth. Beatrice also confronts Catherine with the truth about her relationship with Eddie. She very gently attempts to persuade Catherine that she must break free. Catherine, however, is aware that she will 'kick him in the face' (Act I, p. 42) if she rejects Eddie totally. It may be, of course, that she does not wish to leave the security that her relationship with Eddie gives her.

Like Beatrice, Alfieri is aware of the dangerous nature of the relationship. He also warns Eddie that he must not feel as he does for Catherine. Tactfully he tells him that the relationship has a darker side that must not be allowed to blossom. Eddie reacts angrily and refuses to accept that the relationship is anything other than that of an ordinary relationship between uncle and niece. Every statement made by Alfieri makes it clear that the relationship must end now or it will, eventually, have tragic consequences.

? DID YOU KNOW?

If Rodolpho marries Catherine, an American citizen, he will be allowed to stay in America, legally.

CHECKPOINT 24

Why does Eddie reject Alfieri's comments about the relationship between Catherine and himself?

In the end, of course, Catherine's hostile attack on Eddie is a statement that she has now finally broken free from him. The break in the relationship is now complete.

MANLINESS

Eddie has a very narrow view of what he considers manliness. He may never say it but he feels that manliness consists of knowing one's boundaries and protecting one's territory, territory in which other men are regarded as hostile intruders if they attempt to enter.

CHECKPOINT 25

In what way does Rodolpho's behaviour unsettle Eddie?

Rodolpho's behaviour unsettles Eddie. He does not regard him as a real man as Rodolpho cooks, sings, makes dresses and has platinum hair. He calls him 'Paper Doll', 'canary' and 'a weird' (Act I, p. 35). Beatrice attempts to show him how unreasonable he is being when she suggests that he is jealous of Rodolpho. Eddie rejects this idea.

Beatrice is warm and sensitive. She welcomes the cousins openly. Eddie, however, keeps his distance. He does not regard it as manly to show his emotions in this open way. His comments and questions have usually got an edge to them that make the other **characters** feel uncomfortable or indeed threatened.

Eddie's own masculinity is called into question when Beatrice asks him 'When am I gonna be a wife again, Eddie?' (Act I, p. 36). Later in the play, when he is attempting to regain control in his own home he tells Beatrice that she must never ask questions like this again.

Generally speaking Eddie is a simple man who feels uncomfortable when the boundaries of his manliness are threatened. When he is confused he refuses to accept anything other than his own uncomplicated measure of masculinity.

JUSTICE AND THE LAW

Alfieri, as a lawyer, is aware that the law, despite its limitations, must be upheld. However, he is also aware of the inability of the law to dispense total justice. He feels powerless to intervene when a **character** in the play decides to find justice in his own way – outside the law.

Eddie Carbone is a man who does not understand the reasons for the limitations of the law. Early in the play he asks Beatrice to tell Catherine the story of Vinny Bolzano. In Eddie's eyes and in the eyes of the community Vinny was guilty of injustice and his family ensured that justice was done when he was punished and shunned by the neighbourhood.

There is a feeling that if people always abide by the law then they will have to 'settle for half' (Act II, p. 85). Alfieri seems to be saying that the law is often incapable of satisfying everybody.

Eddie tries to force Alfieri to give him his kind of justice. He believes (or says that he believes) that Rodolpho is going to marry Catherine in order to make him a legal immigrant. He feels that this is unjust and that the law should be capable of making a case against Rodolpho. Alfieri is very rational and unemotional as he informs Eddie that no law has been broken.

The real injustice as far as Eddie is concerned is that Rodolpho, who, according to Eddie, is an effeminate 'weird' guy (p. 35), is taking Catherine for his own and away from Eddie who is, in his own opinion, all that a man should be.

Alfieri warns Eddie that if he betrays the brothers he will be breaching the code of his people and that they will turn against him. Here Alfieri is placing the law against natural justice – he is emphasising that it would be unjust to betray the Italians even if Eddie is actually upholding the law by reporting them.

In the final section of the play Marco demands justice and, as he does so, he echoes the sentiments spoken earlier by Eddie. He says 'The law? All the law is not in a book' (Act II, p. 79). He talks about honour and he talks about blood and about degradation – all of which matter to Marco when he speaks of justice. Again, Alfieri cautions against stepping outside the law.

Throughout the play there is an emphasis on justice, but as Alfieri tells us there is a price to pay for total justice – a price that most people, most of the time, are not prepared to pay. This is why the majority feel that 'it is better to settle for half' (Act II, p. 85).

DID YOU KNOW?

Arthur Miller said that 'the best work anybody ever writes is the work that is on the verge of embarrassing him...'.

CHECK THE NET

There are a number of websites devoted to Arthur Miller and his plays. For example:
**http://www. webenglish teacher.com/ miller.html
http://www. ibiblio.org/miller/**

STRUCTURE

A View from the Bridge is a well-structured play with an uncomplicated shape. The play is in two Acts but within these Acts there are a number of easily defined divisions which are controlled by the lawyer, Alfieri. Alfieri is essential to the **structure** of the play. He opens and closes the play and at other times we see him as Arthur Miller's mouthpiece moving the action quickly onwards.

EXAMINER'S SECRET

Write about the atmosphere and mood created by the dramatist.

All the action revolves around Eddie Carbone. His **character** controls the drama. When he is calm and friendly, the **atmosphere** is likewise. When he is tense and hostile the atmosphere is uncomfortable. There are a number of flashpoints in the two Acts which echo one another. The controlled hostility at the end of Act I (when Eddie shows Rodolpho how to box and Marco indirectly challenges Eddie) is developed into unpleasant hostility at the beginning of Act II when Eddie kisses Catherine and Rodolpho. The final explosive violence at the end of the drama is justified when we consider what has gone before.

The themes of the play – incest, justice, manliness (see **Themes**) – are woven into the action and are always part of the fabric of the drama. Arthur Miller moves the action and the themes simply and forcefully through the play until he reaches the final tragic scene.

CHARACTERS

EDDIE

Eddie is the main **character** in the play and every significant act in the drama is connected to him. He is forceful, energetic and obsessive. He is capable of self-delusion on a grand scale. He is also, however, a character who can show warmth and some generosity.

He is protective towards Catherine at the beginning of the play and he does not wish her to expose herself to the attentions of the men of the neighbourhood. He comments on her clothes and the way she looks. His interest in Catherine soon becomes obsessive and is obviously unnatural. He lays down rules for Catherine to live by and he finds it impossible to accept that she should have a life of her own apart from her relationship with him.

Eddie is a man who has few interests outside the family and, in the end, no interests, apart from himself and his relationship with Catherine.

Eddie's changes of mood can be quite sharp. Even when joking about the sacrifices he has to make for the coming of Beatrice's cousins there is an unpleasant edge to his comments. It is difficult for any of the characters to be completely at ease with Eddie. There are few moments in the play when he is not in conflict. Much of their time is spent in attempting to placate him.

Before the cousins arrive Eddie creates the impression that he is the authority in his own household. He lays down the rules and it is to him that Beatrice and Catherine must refer if they wish to deviate from the routine that has been established. When the play opens we sense an air of unease because Catherine and Beatrice are unsure of what Eddie's reaction will be when he is told about Catherine's job.

Eddie's reaction to Rodolpho demonstrates how emotionally unstable and irrational he is. His jealousy of the young man drives him to accuse him of being homosexual, effeminate and he also accuses him that he is only interested in Catherine because she could be his passport to achieving full American citizenship.

Self-interest is one of Eddie's great motivating factors. He is deeply aware of the horrific nature of betraying an immigrant to the authorities and yet, when his own comfortable relationship with Catherine is threatened, he is quite prepared to break this code of honour. Later, he will not accept the truth when Marco accuses him of betrayal and, instead, tries to plead for support against Marco's 'lies'.

In the end Eddie realises that his honourable 'name' (Act II, p. 82) is at stake. He has betrayed his name and he has lost the respect of all those who know him and therefore he has no option but to face Marco in mortal combat. Perhaps, in the end, he gains some dignity

Forceful
Obsessive
Warm
Protective
Irrational

EXAMINER'S SECRET
Try producing a single revision sheet for each of the key characters and themes. Set it out in the form of a diagram with essential quotations and some *phrases of your own*.

in the way he dies. In any case, as Alfieri says, Eddie 'allowed himself to be wholly known' (Act II, p. 85).

BEATRICE

Beatrice is loving and caring. She is capable of taking an overview of the situations as they occur. She is often the mediator when Eddie's aggressiveness creates hostile situations. She can, however, be quite assertive when she feels the occasion demands. It is she who attempts to warn Eddie that his relationship with Catherine is not within acceptable bounds. Catherine is also warned by Beatrice that she is contributing to Eddie's infatuation. Beatrice feels that Eddie does not behave as a husband should and she indicates that he has not made love to her for some time. She knows her rights as a wife and she is not prepared to let Eddie ignore these rights especially as it seems that his infatuation with Catherine is the root cause.

Loving
Caring
Mediator
Assertive

**Represents reason
and sanity**

Beatrice is the thread of reason that runs throughout the play. She is always able to rise above any situation created by Eddie and she is always prepared to do whatever is necessary to recreate sanity in their lives even to the extent of refusing to go to Catherine's wedding because Eddie does not want her to. She is the one who is always attempting to pull Eddie back from the edge of darkness. And when he does slip over the edge she is the one who is there to comfort him.

CATHERINE

Catherine is a lively young women who is eager to experience the world. She is innocent and open, always ready to love and be loved. However, she has had no real experience until Rodolpho enters her life. Until now her security has been bound to her relationship with Eddie and Beatrice. She is genuinely unaware that there is anything improper in her relationship with Eddie and is horrified when Beatrice suggests that there might be more to the bond than she realises.

She is heavily influenced by Eddie and, for this reason, she is doubtful about Rodolpho's motives in marrying her. She quickly accepts his assurances, however, and this is the moment when she abandons herself to him. She now accepts her love for Rodolpho without restraint. She takes sides against Eddie and is quite vehement in her condemnation of his actions when he betrays Rodolpho and Marco. This is the point in the play where she shows a strength of character that has not been in evidence before. However, any strength this might have given her evaporates in the final moments of the play when she murmurs her heartfelt regret for her part in Eddie's tragic end.

Lively
Innocent
Open
Initially influenced by Eddie
Gains independence

MARCO

When he enters, Marco is seen as the stronger of the two brothers. He is only too well aware of his obligations to Eddie and this is why he is happy to suggest to Rodolpho that his brother should not behave in a manner that will upset Eddie. His strong sense of responsibility to his wife and family is obvious and is, therefore, the only reason he has come to America. He gives the impression that he thinks before he acts.

However, he has a strong sense of right and wrong and an even stronger sense of justice. When he sees Eddie hitting his brother he is quick to show Eddie that he, the stronger man, will be there to defend Rodolpho if necessary. When his mind is made up he is totally focused – he employs tunnel vision.

Responsible
Strong sense of justice
Focused
Strong

Marco's intention to punish Eddie is not a selfish one, he feels that it is his duty to do so. If the law will not help him he will take the law into his own hands. His sense of morality is very clear. We are not absolutely certain that Marco would have killed Eddie if Eddie had not pulled a knife on him but, having said that, Arthur Miller does not allow Marco to express any sorrow or regret for the death of Eddie. Marco is the **character** about whom Arthur Miller tells us least. He is the **antagonist** in the play and the Sicilian avenging angel that Alfieri hints at in his comment to the audience.

RODOLPHO

Rodolpho makes an immediate impact when he enters. Catherine and Beatrice find him an attractive young man and his lively sense of humour endears him to the audience. He is delighted to be in America as his very first line makes clear. His command of the

**Attractive
Humorous
Intelligent
Talented
Sensitive**

language is impressive even though Arthur Miller makes it obvious that English is not his first language. His use of words and images shows a lightness of touch that betrays an intelligent mind at work. He is a man of many talents – many of which are sneered at by Eddie. He can cook, he can sing and he can make clothes. Eddie's hostility upsets him mainly because he cannot understand why Eddie should dislike him.

Rodolpho, more than any other **character**, has a love of life in all its forms and he has a tendency to influence other characters with his ebullience. Catherine falls in love with him very quickly and Rodolpho's love for her is genuine and powerful. This is nowhere more evident than at the beginning of Act II when the audience hears his reasons for staying in America with Catherine as his bride.

It is interesting to note the change in roles between Rodolpho and Marco as the play progresses. At first Marco is seen as the strong one, the leader, the 'reasonable' brother. However, at the end of the play we see Rodolpho as the thoughtful, sensitive young man who has the vision to see what terrible consequences will result from the battle of wills between Marco and Eddie. He attempts to persuade Marco not to harm Eddie, he apologises to Eddie for his behaviour and finally tries to warn Eddie that Marco is in no mood to capitulate or compromise. All this shows the audience that Rodolpho is a sensitive, intelligent character who feels a sense of responsibility for those close to him.

ALFIERI

Alfieri is a narrator, commentator and sometimes a character in the play itself. He can sense the terrible events that are about to happen but is powerless to prevent them (see **chorus**). He dispenses information and advice and, most emphatically, explains the law and its boundaries. It is he who attempts to place the events of the drama in context and explain to the audience that conflicts such as those related in the play occur throughout Italian and Sicilian history.

Alfieri talks about it being 'better to settle for half' (Act II, p. 85) and about liking that better because, quite often, the search for absolute justice results in unacceptable consequences. He realises that the law is limited and cannot deal with every human problem fully. He explains the boundaries to both Marco and Eddie but, even though in his heart he knows they will ignore what he has said to them, he cannot take further action to prevent the conflict.

Arthur Miller has not drawn Alfieri as a full 'flesh and blood' character even though there are times when we feel sympathy for his predicament. Alfieri's role is to oversee the action and remain objective throughout. The audience can see, at the end of the play, that Alfieri does have sympathy for Eddie and even some admiration for him because 'he allowed himself to be wholly known' (Act II, p. 85). And there, finally, we have Alfieri's most important role. He offers the audience universal concepts to think about as they leave the theatre.

Narrator
Commentator
Oversees action
Objective
Sympathetic

LANGUAGE AND STYLE

There are a variety of language forms in *A View from the Bridge*. The audience hears the educated, controlled dialogue of Alfieri, the aggressive uneducated speech of Eddie, the intelligent, attractive conversations of Rodolpho, the heavy serious tones of Marco, the lively searching words of Catherine and finally the quiet, serious language of Beatrice. Arthur Miller's **dialogue** is, in turn, powerful, economical, colourful and dramatic.

ALFIERI – EDUCATED, CONTROLLED DIALOGUE

The language of Alfieri is meditative and helps the audience to think about the issues which Miller feels are important. His leisurely style draws the audience into his story and helps to maintain a relationship with them throughout the play. In the opening lines he uses the pronoun 'you' to indicate that he is talking directly to us. The use of 'you' also shows that he is the medium between audience and the characters.

His wry sense of humour at the beginning of Act I when he refers to himself as an object of superstition and again at the beginning of Act II when he mentions the case of Scotch Whisky slipping 'from a net while being unloaded' (Act II, p. 59) endears his audience to him. It

 CHECK THE BOOK

The play *The Caucasian Chalk Circle* (Penguin, 1949) by Bertolt Brecht should be read if only for an examination of the function of 'The Singer' who, like Alfieri, is a narrator and commentator – one of whose functions is to offer ideas to the audience to set them thinking!

CHECK THE FILM

Whenever possible the student should attempt to see plays in live performance. If this is not possible there are a number of filmed versions of Arthur Miller's plays especially *Death of a Salesman* and *The Crucible*. Unfortunately at the present time, a film version of *A View from the Bridge* is not available on video. There are also a number of audio productions which are very useful for home and classroom use.

also shows a detachment from the events taking place which allows the character to take an objective view of the whole proceedings. Because he is also a **character** in the play he speaks in a different mode when communicating with the other characters. He speaks as a lawyer but he also speaks as a friend giving sound advice. Occasionally there is a huge sweep to the language used by Alfieri particularly at the beginning of Act I when he says:

> ... every few years there is still a case, and as the parties tell me what the trouble is, the flat air in my office suddenly washes in with the green scent of the sea   (Act I, p. 12)

and he goes on to link this case with another in Italy more than two thousand years before. Using colourful locations e.g. 'Calabria' and 'Syracuse' (Act I, p. 12) he gives the scene an importance and relevance that indicates that the events are timeless and are no respectors of boundaries. There are echoes of this style in Act II, 'But I will never forget how dark the room became when he looked at me; his eyes were like tunnels' (p. 65) and in the final speech when he focuses on the tragedy that is Eddie's and tries to makes some sense of it:

> ... I tremble, for I confess that something perversely pure calls to me from his memory – not purely good, but himself purely, for he allowed himself to be wholly known and for that I think I will love him more that all my sensible clients.   (Act II, p. 85)

RAW POWER OF EDDIE'S SPEECH

Eddie's dialogue couldn't be in greater contrast to Alfieri's speech. We hear his limited language skills but even so there is often a raw power evident in what he says. He speaks in short, uncomplicated sentences which do not allow him to develop his thoughts. His language can often be brutally unpleasant, e.g. when he orders Rodolpho to leave after he sees him coming out of Catherine's bedroom and at the end of the play when he accuses Marco of taking away his name.

He often does not complete words or sentences or, indeed, he runs words together: 'Where you goin' all dressed up?' (Act I, p. 13), 'lemme see in the back' (Act I, p. 13). Even so, he does occasionally express himself in a colourful way when he tells Catherine that she is 'walkin' wavy' (Act I, p. 14) and that the men's heads are 'turnin' like windmills' (Act I, p. 14). His language nearly always shows a fiercely narrow focus. Eddie is not capable of opening out. At the end of the play he keeps on repeating over and over again that he wants his name back.

The rawness of the language lacks any subtlety and it is this primitive use of words that creates the tension at the end of Act I, the viciousness when he tells Rodolpho to leave and, finally, the tragic events at the end of the play.

DIALOGUE

Arthur Miller sometimes uses dialogue to show the lack of real communication between the characters. A very powerful example of this is when Beatrice accuses Eddie of not being a proper husband to her:

Beatrice:	No, everything ain't great with me.
Eddie:	No?
Beatrice:	No. But I got other worries.
Eddie:	Yeah. [*He is already weakening.*]
Beatrice:	Yeah, you want me to tell you?
Eddie: [*in retreat*]	Why? What worries you got?
Beatrice:	When am I gonna be a wife again, Eddie?
	(Act I, pp. 35–6)

Eddie is refusing to respond to her probing because he does not want to recognise what he feels for Catherine and his lack of affection for Beatrice. He speaks in short bursts which he hopes will prevent further scrutiny by Beatrice. He says 'No?', 'Yeah', 'Why, what worries you got?'. The last example is not an invitation to speak but a rhetorical question to silence her. When Beatrice continues relentlessly he stops the questions with a blunt 'I don't want to talk about it' and later, even more brutally, 'I can't talk about it!' and 'I got nothin' to say about it!' (Act I, p. 36).

EXAMINER'S SECRET
An A-grade student is able to provide a detailed account of language features, or structured patterns, to support a conclusion about the author's intentions.

In the final section of Act I, Eddie speaks to Rodolpho as if he is complimenting him by comparing Rodolpho's talent with his own lack of skill. He repeats his list of Rodolpho's talents – three times he lists them – superficially to show how much he admires him but in reality he wants Rodolpho to be seen as effeminate and not as a real man. About the coffee that Catherine offers to make he says, 'Make it nice and strong' (Act I, p. 56) indicating that he, a real man, likes his coffee strong.

POWER THROUGH ECONOMY

EXAMINER'S SECRET

A feature of A-grade writing on literature is the ability to see two possible interpretations and to support a preference for one of them.

We see the power and economy of Arthur Miller's language in the final page of Act I. Marco does not need to tell Eddie that he is the stronger. His actions (indicated by Miller's stage directions) and his brief invitation to Eddie: 'Can you lift this chair?' (p. 57) are sufficient to create a very intense movement which speaks volumes about the change of **atmosphere** and the change in the way characters relate to one another.

At the beginning of Act II (and indeed throughout the play) Rodolpho's conversation is soft, comforting and all-embracing except for the moments when he is at odds with Eddie. He is obviously a generous romantic. His dialogue betrays an open, honest person. His warmth and protectiveness are seen when he attempts to liberate Catherine from Eddie:

> Catherine. If I take in my hands a little bird. And she grows and wishes to fly. But I will not let her out of my hands because I love her so much, is that right for me to do? I don't say you must hate him; but anyway you must go, mustn't you? Catherine?'
> (Act II, p. 63)

The use of 'Catherine' at the beginning and at the end is significant. The first mention of her name draws her in. It shows intimacy. The final 'Catherine' is a question asking for her agreement and therefore for her acceptance of their relationship and an end to the claustrophobic entanglement with Eddie.

Marco's conversation tells the audience that he is a serious man who is earnest about his responsibilities. His language informs us of his thoughtful nature. He is also very passionate and can be brutally direct when he feels an injustice has been done. At the end of the play he speaks to Eddie a mere five times but each comment is full of venom and intensity.

DIALOGUE OF CONFRONTATION

In the end it is Eddie's uneducated American working-class conversation that sounds the most realistic of all the characters. His words are anchored in reality and we realise that he speaks the truth as he sees it. His vision of the truth is twisted but is, nevertheless, true for him. His dialogue is never far away from confrontation and builds relentlessly to the inevitable tragedy at the end of the play.

It is worth looking at the way tension is built and maintained in the dialogue during the final moments of the play. Confrontation is built on confrontation. Beatrice's conversation is soothing, attempting to calm things down but Eddie does not listen. His conversation is shot through with comments that do not allow compromise: 'Didn't you hear what I told you? You walk out that door to the wedding you ain't comin' back here, Beatrice' (Act II, p. 80).

Later Marco is in the same uncompromising mood: 'Animal! You go on your knees to me!' (Act II, p. 84). Eddie insists that he must have his good name restored: 'You lied about me, Marco. Now say it. Come on now, say it!' (Act II, p. 84).

The dialogue carries with it the inevitability of tragedy that may shock, but does not surprise, the audience.

DID YOU KNOW?

A View from the Bridge was banned in Britain by the Lord Chamberlain in 1956 because of its homosexual overtones.

Now take a break!

RESOURCES

How to use quotations

One of the secrets of success in writing essays is the way you use quotations. There are five basic principles:

❶ Put inverted commas at the beginning and end of the quotation.

❷ Write the quotation exactly as it appears in the original.

❸ Do not use a quotation that repeats what you have just written.

❹ Use the quotation so that it fits into your sentence.

❺ Keep the quotation as short as possible.

Quotations should be used to develop the line of thought in your essays. Your comment should not duplicate what is in your quotation. For example:

Eddie Carbone tells Catherine that she must not trust anybody, 'I only ask you one thing – don't trust nobody' (Act I, p. 21)

Far more effective is to write:

Eddie Carbone tells Catherine to 'trust nobody' (Act I, p. 21)

Always lay out the lines as they appear in the text. For example:

Alfieri is worried about Eddie:
'His eyes were like tunnels; my first thought was that he had committed a crime' (Act I, p. 45)

However, the most sophisticated way of using the writer's words is to embed them into your sentence:

Alfieri feels that compromise is better and that 'now we settle for half' (Act I, p. 85)

When you use quotations in this way, you are demonstating the ability to use text as evidence to support your ideas – not simply including words from the original to prove you have read it.

COURSEWORK ESSAY

Set aside an hour or so at the start of your work to plan what you have to do.

- List all the points you feel are needed to cover the task. Collect page references of information and quotations that will support what you have to say. A helpful tool is the highlighter pen: this saves painstaking copying and enables you to target precisely what you want to use.

- Focus on what you consider to be the main points of the essay. Try to sum up your argument in a single sentence, which could be the closing sentence of your essay. Depending on the essay title, it could be a statement about a character: Marco's decision to punish Eddie is not a selfish one, he feels that it is his duty to do so; an opinion about setting: The language used by Beatrice, Catherine and Eddie is incisive and colloquial; or a judgement on a theme: One of the main themes in *A View from the Bridge* is justice because Eddie and Marco search for their own type of justice in different ways.

- Make a short essay plan. Use the first paragraph to introduce the argument you wish to make. In the following paragraphs develop this argument with details, examples and other possible points of view. Sum up your argument in the last paragraph. Check you have answered the question.

- Write the essay, remembering all the time the central point you are making.

- On completion, go back over what you have written to eliminate careless errors and improve expression. Read it aloud to yourself, or, if you are feeling more confident, to relative or friend.

If you can, try to type you essay, using a word processor. This will allow you to correct and improve your writing without spoiling its appearance.

EXAMINER'S SECRET

In a typical examination you might use as many as eight quotations.

SITTING THE EXAMINATION

EXAMINER'S SECRET

If you cannot choose between two questions, jot down a plan for each to help you decide – it may be that what appeared to be the most straightforward question is more difficult than you thought.

Examination papers are carefully designed to give you the opportunity to do your best. Follow these handy hints for exam success:

BEFORE YOU START

- Make sure you know the subject of the examination so that you are properly prepared and equipped.

- You need to be comfortable and free from distractions. Inform the invigilator if anything is off-putting, e.g. a shaky desk.

- Read the instructions, or rubric, on the front of the examination paper. You should know by now what you have to do but check to reassure yourself.

- Observe the time allocation – and follow it carefully. If they recommend 60 minutes for Question 1 and 30 minutes for Question 2, it is because Question 1 carries twice as many marks.

- Consider the mark allocation. You should write a longer response for 4 marks than for 2 marks.

WRITING YOUR RESPONSES

- Use the questions to structure your response, e.g. question: 'The endings of X's poems are always particularly significant. Explain their importance with reference to two poems.' The first part of your answer will describe the ending of the first poem; the second part will look at the ending of the second poem; the third part will be an explanation of the significance of the two endings.

- Write a brief draft outline of your response.

- A typical 30-minute examination essay is probably between 400 and 600 words in length.

- Keep your writing legible and easy to read, using paragraphs to show the structure of your answers.

- Spend a couple of minutes afterwards quickly checking for obvious errors.

WHEN YOU HAVE FINISHED

- Don't be downhearted – if you found the examination difficult, it is probably because you really worked at the questions. Let's face it, they are not meant to be easy!

- Don't pay too much attention to what your friends have to say about the paper. Everyone's experience is different and no two people ever give the same answers.

IMPROVE YOUR GRADE

You have spent some time studying *A View from the Bridge* and, with the help of these York Notes, you have a good understanding of the novel. Coursework essays and examination questions give you an opportunity to show your knowledge – they are not meant to catch you out or make you look silly. By following some simple guidelines you will be able to write with confidence and easily improve your grade. The advice that comes next will help you answer examination questions but may also be useful with other types of writing about the play.

Your potential grades in any examination can be improved. Your paper is marked according to a marking scheme applied to all candidates and no examiner knows in advance your level of achievement. All candidates start with a blank answer booklet.

The commonest problem is a simple one: failure to answer the question. Do not begin writing until you know precisely what you want to say. Otherwise, it is far too easy to go off the point and start waffling. A good idea is to look back occasionally to the question and check that you are still answering it.

AN EXAMPLE

Let's look at the question **'What compels Eddie to abandon his beliefs and values?'** and consider how different students might answer it.

6 EXAMINER'S SECRET

Always read the whole examination paper before you start writing.

A **C-grade answer** would show the following:

- Clear <u>understanding</u> of emotions, relationships and ideas
- Precise use of details from the play to support comments made
- Familiarity with dramatic technique and reasons for its use

A **D-grade answer**, however, would show:

- Familiarity with emotions, relationships and ideas
- Some use of details to support comments made
- Some knowledge of dramatic techniques

IMPROVING FROM A D TO A C GRADE

EXAMINER'S SECRET

As you write, check that you are still answering the question. It is surprisingly easy to start well and drift off the subject entirely.

The following represents one approach which would help a student to gain a C grade:

Introduction

In this first paragraph you have to show immediate understanding of what is required and also understanding of Eddie's motives. The following is an example of how you might write an introduction:

> **Near the beginning of the play Eddie asks Beatrice to tell Catherine the story of Vinny Bolzano. He does so in order to impress on Catherine his belief that nobody should 'snitch' on their friends and neighbours to the authorities. When he does betray the cousins to the Immigration Authorities he does so because he desperately needs to destroy the relationship between Rodolpho and Catherine.**

Development

You should now address the following points:

- Eddie's conversation with Beatrice about the cousins and his co-operative nature which shows that he has no objections to their visit.
- Eddie's reaction to Rodolpho's singing and Alfieri's comment, 'Now, as the weeks passed, there was a future, there was a trouble that would not go away' (Act I, p. 34).

- Alfieri's conversation with Eddie which shows that Eddie's obsession with Rodolpho is growing, his embarrassment and jealousy are interfering with his clear thinking.

- The clash at the end of Act I between Marco and Eddie and the lead up to the confrontation.

- Eddie's reaction to Rodolpho when he comes out of Catherine's bedroom, his conversation with Alfieri and his telephone call to the Immigration Authorities. You should comment here that Eddie has finally decided that his interests are more important than doing the right thing and that his beliefs and values are no longer important.

- The final act of defiance when Eddie deludes himself that Marco is wrong and he is right (page 83 to the end).

Conclusion

Your conclusion might read something like this:

Eddie's obsession with Catherine and consequently with Rodolpho's and Catherine's relationship drives him over the edge. From the moment he sees Catherine's attraction to Beatrice's cousin he can no longer think logically. It is this that pushes him to forget his loyalty to Beatrice and the two men and, finally, to betray the immigrants to the authorities.

IMPROVING FROM A C GRADE

We can now look at the question again and this time examine the criteria for an A* grade and a B grade.

An **A*-grade** answer would show the following:

- Clear consistent insight
- Focused analysis of dramatic technique
- Exploration of the dramatist's purpose
- Imaginative personal response
- Close textual analysis

EXAMINER'S SECRET

To do well, you do not have to write at great length: you can get the highest marks with an essay of two sides.

A **B-grade** answer would show:

- A personal response to the text
- Appreciation of emotions and ideas
- Understanding of the dramatist's technique
- Use of details from the play to support comments

TO GAIN AN A* GRADE

The following is an approach that should help you to achieve an A* grade:

Introduction

In the first paragraph you must show an imaginative response and write with some flair.

> **Eddie tells Catherine and Beatrice at the outset that he believes loyalty is very important and anybody who breaks the unwritten code deserves punishment. When he does betray the cousins he makes it quite clear that he feels he himself has been betrayed. Beatrice voices what Eddie does not want hear, his unhealthy relationship with Catherine. It is this relationship, his jealousy of Rodolpho and his own tortured mind which, in the end, force him to abandon his loyalty to the cousins, himself and to his family.**

Development

You could now use the following framework to write the body of your answer:

- Examine Alfieri's opening speech in detail particularly his references to justice and the law. Link this to Eddie's conversation with Beatrice and Catherine when he talks about looking after the cousins. This will demonstrate Eddie's beliefs and values.
- Quote the line, 'Now, as the weeks passed, there was a future, there was a trouble that would not go away' (Act I, p. 34) to establish Eddie's changing mood. Here you should analyse Beatrice's conversation with Eddie (Act I, pp. 35–6). Show the importance of what she says about Eddie's relationship with

DID YOU KNOW?

A View from the Bridge is based on a true story told to Arthur Miller by longshoremen.

Catherine. Your commentary should make clear that already Eddie's attitude to Rodolpho is one of suspicion.

- Again quote from an Alfieri speech (Act I, p. 45) to show Eddie's disintegration, 'His eyes were like tunnels; my first thought was that he had committed a crime, but soon I saw it was only a passion that had moved into his body, like a stranger'.

- It would be worthwhile to comment on Eddie's feelings for Catherine and that it is only now that they are coming to the surface. Rodolpho is the catalyst.

- The final scene in Act I (pp. 52–8) should be analysed in detail to show that Eddie is reaching a watershed. The dramatic moments at the end when Marco confronts him indicate that Eddie has been backed into a corner. In which direction will he move?

- Use the comment by Alfieri to help you to examine how far Eddie has moved away from his original feelings for what is right. Alfieri warns Eddie: 'You won't have a friend in the world, Eddie! Even those who understand will turn against you, even the ones who feel the same will despise you!' (Act II, p. 67). Around this quotation you should discuss Eddie's reaction to Rodolpho when he sees him coming out of Catherine's bedroom and then reporting the cousins to the Immigration Authorities.

- Your answer should now move naturally to look at Eddie's blinkered search for justice and for the return of his 'name' (Act II, p. 82). You could show that the **tragedy** is inevitable because of Eddie's abandonment of his values.

CONCLUSION

The following paragraph is an example of a possible conclusion:

We might feel some disgust at Eddie for the way he has behaved, but, in the end it is difficult to blame him. He has been driven by an obsession that he finds impossible to control. He dare not admit his feelings for Catherine so he has to find other ways of discrediting Rodolpho. It seems obvious in the final moments that he cannot see any way of living and accepting his fate. He has lost Catherine. Beatrice may still love him but part of her despises him and the whole neighbourhood, as Alfieri says, condemns his actions. You could argue, therefore, that

 CHECK THE BOOK

Henrik Ibsen has always been a powerful influence on Arthur Miller, especially when considering the responsibilities of the public and private individuals. *An Enemy of the People* (Viking, 1951) is readily accessible to the young reader and well worth reading.

Eddie engineers his own death at the hands of Marco in order to regain some dignity before finally allowing himself to be destroyed and, therefore, ending the terrible torture that he has created for himself.

SAMPLE ESSAY PLAN

EXAMINER'S SECRET

You are always given credit for writing your essay plans.

A typical essay question on *A View from the Bridge* is followed by a sample essay plan in note form. This does not present the only answer to the question, merely one answer. Do not be afraid to include your own ideas and leave out some of the ones in this sample! Remember that quotations are essential to prove and illustrate the points you make.

Explore the way Arthur Miller writes about justice in *A View from the Bridge*. Write about the characters' search for justice and the feeling that the law is sometimes inadequate.

INTRODUCTION

- Alfieri's thoughts about justice and the law
- Law often inadequate
- Justice not the same for the different characters

PART 1

- The characters' attitude to the law
- No compunction about breaking immigration law or, indeed, other laws
- Betrayal is injustice – Vinny Bolzano
- Irony of Eddie's horror at Vinny's betrayal
- Family mete out their own justice

PART 2

- Eddie's pursuit of justice
- Feels Rodolpho had broken the 'code'
- Alfieri explains the law
- Eddie's frustration that the law cannot give him 'justice'

PART 3

- Eddie's blindness to the injustice he is causing to others
- Not treating Beatrice as a loving husband should
- His obsessive nature smothers Catherine
- His betrayal of the brothers linked to his earlier attitude to Vinny Bolzano

PART 4

- Marco's demands for justice
- Is he more justified than Eddie in demanding vengeance/justice?
- Marco's conversation with Alfieri – compare it with the one Eddie had previously had with the lawyer

PART 5

- Consider Rodolpho's attitude
- Examine his involvement with Eddie and Marco towards end of play
- Is he the one who is prepared to settle for Alfieri's 'half'?

PART 6

- The **climax** of the play and the terrible consequences of two characters' search for justice
- Look at those who lose
- Does anybody win?

CONCLUSION

- General comment on Arthur Miller's treatment of law and justice

 EXAMINER'S SECRET
A candidate who is capable of arriving at unusual, well-supported judgements *independently* is likely to receive the highest marks.

FURTHER QUESTIONS

The following questions require a knowledge of the whole play. You should make a plan like the one on the previous pages before attempting any of the essays.

❶ Compare and contrast the characters of Eddie and Marco.

DID YOU KNOW?

A View from the Bridge started life as a one-Act play in **verse**.

❷ Examine the ideas of manliness, hostility and aggression as they are portrayed in the play. How are these ideas connected?

❸ Discuss the relationship between Eddie and Beatrice. Do you feel that Eddie's feelings for Catherine interfere with this relationship in any way?

❹ What is Alfieri's function in the play?

❺ Compare the characters of Marco and Rodolpho.

❻ Why does Alfieri say that people should 'settle for half'? Is he right to say this?

❼ Write about the relationship between Catherine and Rodolpho. Why does Catherine find Rodolpho attractive?

❽ Discuss the theme of betrayal in *A View from the Bridge*.

❾ How far is Catherine responsible for Eddie's destruction?

❿ Alfieri says Eddie's death is 'useless'. Write your comments on this opinion.

Now take a break!

antagonist the chief opponent of the hero or protagonist in a story; especially used of drama. Thus Marco is the antagonist in *A View from the Bridge*

atmosphere a common term for the mood – moral, sensational, emotional and intellectual – which dominates a piece of writing

autobiography the story of a person's life written by that person. Arthur Miller's autobiography is called *Time Bends* and provides valuable background material for the study of *A View from the Bridge*

character characters are the invented, imaginary persons in a dramatic work which are given human qualities and behaviour

chorus in the tragedies of the ancient Greek playwright Aeschylus the chorus is a group of characters who represent ordinary people in their attitudes to the action which they witness as bystanders and on which they comment. Alfieri describes the situation of the play as it occurs and often reacts to the action. Like the chorus of the Greek Theatre he is powerless to affect events

climax any point of great intensity in a literary work; in a narrative the culminating moment of the action. In *A View from the Bridge* the climax is discovered when Marco turns the knife on Eddie and kills him

colloquialism the use of the kinds of expression and grammar associated with ordinary, everyday speech rather than formal language. The speech of Catherine, Eddie and Beatrice is regarded as colloquial

dialogue the speech and conversation between characters in any kind of literary work

flashback a scene in a play where the narrative suddenly returns to something that has happened in the past

full-length prose a play that is written in plain speech e.g. the final version of *A View from the Bridge*

genre the term for a kind of literature. The three major genres of literature are poetry, drama and the novel (prose); these kinds may be subdivided into many other genres such as narrative verse, tragedy, comedy, short story and so on

irony a way of writing in which what is meant is opposite to what the words seem to express. Dramatic irony occurs when the audience is aware of circumstances that are hidden from the characters in the play

melodrama the most common critical use of the word 'melodrama' or 'melodramatic' is to characterise any kind of writing which relies on sensational happenings, violent action and improbable events. Some critics see *A View from the Bridge* as melodramatic because of its violent ending

pathos moments in works of art which evoke strong feelings of pity and sorrow are said to have this quality

protagonist in Greek drama the principal character and actor. Now used almost synonymously with 'hero' to refer to the leading character in a play. Eddie is the protagonist in *A View from the Bridge* though we might argue about the term 'hero' when referring to him

structure the overall principle of organisation in a work of literature

style the characteristic manner in which a writer
expresses him/herself, or the particular manner of
an individual literary work

tragedy possibly the most easily recognised **genre**
in literature and certainly one of the most
discussed. Basically a tragedy traces the career and
downfall of an individual and shows in this
downfall both the capacities and the limitations of
human life. The protagonist may be superhuman, a
monarch or, in the modern age, an ordinary
person. *A View from the Bridge* is regarded as a
tragedy by some critics but some also regard it as a
melodrama

verse play a play that is written in the poetic form
usually in blank verse (i.e. it does not rhyme but it
has rhythm) e.g. the original version of *A View
from the Bridge*

CHECKPOINT HINTS/ANSWERS

CHECKPOINT 1 Justice is the quality of treating people fairly and reasonably.

CHECKPOINT 2 Eddie behaves as he believes a father should behave towards a daughter but his possessiveness does not seem natural.

CHECKPOINT 3 The family are a little worried by the fact that they will have illegal immigrants under the roof.

CHECKPOINT 4 Eddie is unhappy when he hears that Catherine is going to work.

CHECKPOINT 5 The story about Vinny Bolzano is important because it shows the **irony** of Eddie's betrayal later in the play.

CHECKPOINT 6 Superficially it seems that Eddie is worried that Rodolpho will be discovered by the Immigration Authorities. In reality, however, he is jealous of Catherine's interest in Rodolpho's singing.

CHECKPOINT 7 Eddie is jealous because Rodolpho seems to have all the qualities that appeal to Catherine.

CHECKPOINT 8 Eddie is attempting to discredit Rodolpho.

CHECKPOINT 9 Catherine is afraid that Eddie's suggestion may be true, that Rodolpho may be using his relationship with her for his own ends.

CHECKPOINT 10 Beatrice realises that Catherine is not aware of the long-term implications of her relationship with Eddie.

CHECKPOINT 11 Eddie wants Alfieri to prove that Rodolpho's actions are not within the law.

CHECKPOINT 12 Alfieri knows that he is giving Eddie advice that will prevent a tragedy, yet Eddie is ignoring this advice.

CHECKPOINT 13 Eddie is saying that in America girls should be treated with respect. He says that Rodolpho is breaking the code by not asking his permission when taking Catherine to the cinema.

CHECKPOINT 14 Alfieri speaks directly to the audience about events in the play and he is also a character in his own right.

CHECKPOINT 15 The audience knows that Marco is the more powerful through his actions and facial expression. The look that Eddie sees makes it clear that Marco is capable of breaking Eddie.

CHECKPOINT 16 Marco is physically stronger than Eddie and it seems that he is mentally and morally more powerful also.

CHECKPOINT 17 Rodolpho reassures Catherine by being totally honest with her about his intentions and about his reasons for becoming an American citizen.

CHECKPOINT 18 Rodolpho is focused, comforting to Catherine and aware of the dangers to Catherine if she continues to stay in Eddie's shadow.

CHECKPOINT 19 Beatrice attempts to bring some peace and sanity to the household. She tries to show Eddie and Catherine that what is happening between them will have repercussions.

CHECKPOINT 20 Eddie has earlier criticised people who betray their family (see Checkpoint 5).

CHECKPOINT HINTS/ANSWERS

CHECKPOINT 21 Alfieri tells the audience that it is better to 'settle for half' (p. 85) because tragedy often results when people try to achieve total justice.

CHECKPOINT 22 Beatrice tries to make Eddie see that he is smothering Catherine.

CHECKPOINT 23 Eddie tries to discredit Rodolpho by pointing to his supposed 'effeminate' qualities.

CHECKPOINT 24 Eddie realises that if he accepts Alfieri's comments he will not be able to live with himself.

CHECKPOINT 25 One reason may be that Eddie feels that Rodolpho is not a 'real man' but the most likely reason is that he sees Rodolpho as a threat.

TEST ANSWERS

TEST YOURSELF (ACT I: PART ONE)

1 Alfieri

2 Catherine

3 Beatrice

4 Catherine

5 Rodolpho

6 Marco

7 Catherine

TEST YOURSELF (ACT I: PART TWO)

1 Alfieri

2 Eddie

3 Eddie

4 Catherine

5 Rodolpho

6 Catherine

7 Eddie

TEST YOURSELF (ACT I: PART THREE)

1 Alfieri

2 Eddie

3 Alfieri

4 Eddie

5 Rodolpho

6 Eddie

7 Rodolpho

TEST YOURSELF (ACT II: PART ONE)

1 Rodolpho

2 Rodolpho

3 Alfieri

4 Beatrice

5 Eddie

6 Rodolpho

7 Marco

TEST YOURSELF (ACT II: PART TWO)

1 Catherine

2 Catherine

3 Eddie

4 Rodolpho

5 Eddie

6 Beatrice

7 Marco

Maya Angelou
I Know Why the Caged Bird Sings

Jane Austen
Pride and Prejudice

Alan Ayckbourn
Absent Friends

Elizabeth Barrett Browning
Selected Poems

Robert Bolt
A Man for All Seasons

Harold Brighouse
Hobson's Choice

Charlotte Brontë
Jane Eyre

Emily Brontë
Wuthering Heights

Shelagh Delaney
A Taste of Honey

Charles Dickens
David Copperfield
Great Expectations
Hard Times
Oliver Twist

Roddy Doyle
Paddy Clarke Ha Ha Ha

George Eliot
Silas Marner
The Mill on the Floss

Anne Frank
The Diary of a Young Girl

William Golding
Lord of the Flies

Oliver Goldsmith
She Stoops to Conquer

Willis Hall
The Long and the Short and the Tall

Thomas Hardy
Far from the Madding Crowd

The Mayor of Casterbridge
Tess of the d'Urbervilles
The Withered Arm and other Wessex Tales

L.P. Hartley
The Go-Between

Seamus Heaney
Selected Poems

Susan Hill
I'm the King of the Castle

Barry Hines
A Kestrel for a Knave

Louise Lawrence
Children of the Dust

Harper Lee
To Kill a Mockingbird

Laurie Lee
Cider with Rosie

Arthur Miller
The Crucible
A View from the Bridge

Robert O'Brien
Z for Zachariah

Frank O'Connor
My Oedipus Complex and Other Stories

George Orwell
Animal Farm

J.B. Priestley
An Inspector Calls
When We Are Married

Willy Russell
Educating Rita
Our Day Out

J.D. Salinger
The Catcher in the Rye

William Shakespeare
Henry IV Part 1
Henry V
Julius Caesar

Macbeth
The Merchant of Venice
A Midsummer Night's Dream
Much Ado About Nothing
Romeo and Juliet
The Tempest
Twelfth Night

George Bernard Shaw
Pygmalion

Mary Shelley
Frankenstein

R.C. Sherriff
Journey's End

Rukshana Smith
Salt on the snow

John Steinbeck
Of Mice and Men

Robert Louis Stevenson
Dr Jekyll and Mr Hyde

Jonathan Swift
Gulliver's Travels

Robert Swindells
Daz 4 Zoe

Mildred D. Taylor
Roll of Thunder, Hear My Cry

Mark Twain
Huckleberry Finn

James Watson
Talking in Whispers

Edith Wharton
Ethan Frome

William Wordsworth
Selected Poems

A Choice of Poets
Mystery Stories of the Nineteenth Century including The Signalman
Nineteenth Century Short Stories
Poetry of the First World War
Six Women Poets

Margaret Atwood
Cat's Eye
The Handmaid's Tale

Jane Austen
Emma
Mansfield Park
Persuasion
Pride and Prejudice
Sense and Sensibility

Alan Bennett
Talking Heads

William Blake
*Songs of Innocence and of
Experience*

Charlotte Brontë
Jane Eyre
Villette

Emily Brontë
Wuthering Heights

Angela Carter
Nights at the Circus

Geoffrey Chaucer
The Franklin's Prologue and Tale
The Miller's Prologue and Tale
*The Prologue to the Canterbury
Tales*
*The Wife of Bath's Prologue and
Tale*

Samuel Coleridge
Selected Poems

Joseph Conrad
Heart of Darkness

Daniel Defoe
Moll Flanders

Charles Dickens
Bleak House
Great Expectations
Hard Times

Emily Dickinson
Selected Poems

John Donne
Selected Poems

Carol Ann Duffy
Selected Poems

George Eliot
Middlemarch
The Mill on the Floss

T.S. Eliot
Selected Poems
The Waste Land

F. Scott Fitzgerald
The Great Gatsby

E.M. Forster
A Passage to India

Brian Friel
Translations

Thomas Hardy
Jude the Obscure
The Mayor of Casterbridge
The Return of the Native
Selected Poems
Tess of the d'Urbervilles

Seamus Heaney
*Selected Poems from 'Opened
Ground'*

Nathaniel Hawthorne
The Scarlet Letter

Homer
The Iliad
The Odyssey

Aldous Huxley
Brave New World

Kazuo Ishiguro
The Remains of the Day

Ben Jonson
The Alchemist

James Joyce
Dubliners

John Keats
Selected Poems

Christopher Marlowe
Doctor Faustus
Edward II

Arthur Miller
Death of a Salesman

John Milton
Paradise Lost Books I & II

Toni Morrison
Beloved

George Orwell
Nineteen Eighty-Four

Sylvia Plath
Selected Poems

Alexander Pope
*Rape of the Lock & Selected
Poems*

William Shakespeare
Antony and Cleopatra
As You Like It
Hamlet
Henry IV Part I
King Lear
Macbeth
Measure for Measure
The Merchant of Venice
A Midsummer Night's Dream
Much Ado About Nothing
Othello
Richard II
Richard III
Romeo and Juliet
The Taming of the Shrew
The Tempest
Twelfth Night
The Winter's Tale

George Bernard Shaw
Saint Joan

Mary Shelley
Frankenstein

Jonathan Swift
*Gulliver's Travels and A Modest
Proposal*

Alfred Tennyson
Selected Poems

Virgil
The Aeneid

Alice Walker
The Color Purple

Oscar Wilde
The Importance of Being Earnest

Tennessee Williams
A Streetcar Named Desire

Jeanette Winterson
Oranges Are Not the Only Fruit

John Webster
The Duchess of Malfi

Virginia Woolf
To the Lighthouse

W.B. Yeats
Selected Poems
Metaphysical Poets